The
Forgotten
Insurance

**What Your Financial
Advisor Should Be
Telling You About
Protecting Your
Most Valuable Asset**

By: Greg Nelson

The Forgotten Insurance

Find us on the World Wide Web at:

www.theforgotteninsurance.com

Table of Contents

Table of Contents

Preface

We both stood there, staring in disbelief at the results of my daughter's latest visit to the doctor. It was a result that, in my worst nightmares, I never wanted to see happen to any of my family: CANCER.

Having helped countless families get disability income protection, and having seen the effects of disability on both myself and clients, I had insisted that my daughter get this invaluable protection. But I never imagined that, at such a young age she would need it, even for a partial disability.

 My daughter broke into tears after reading the results. At thirty-one years of age, and a mother of three children, how was she going to be able to go through the treatment and still be able to help her husband and kids? At this point, we hadn't even started to consider the impact that this would have on her family, financially, since she worked for me as an assistant and was generating over half of the family's income.

"What are you going to do?" I asked, still in a daze over what was going on.

"I have an appointment with the oncologist next week to see where we go from here." Megan said between sobs.

"Take the time you need to care for yourself. Mom and I will help with your family."

Even though I helped Megan get disability insurance two years ago, it was only now sinking in how glad we were that she had it.

When I first began working in the insurance industry, I had purchased a disability policy; not because I thought that I would ever use it, but because a wise mentor of mine once said,

"You can't sell what you don't own."

So, I purchased a policy so I could sell the same to my clients and not be ashamed for not having one myself.

As I sat with Megan, waiting to learn the results of her tests, I was reminded of how disability income protection had provided tax-free income to my family and I. This income allowed me to recover from Meniere's Disease, instead of neglecting my health to focus on how to put food on the table for my family.

When I went into the emergency room with severe pain in my neck, I knew something wasn't right but I never expected what was coming next.

Megan and I read my doctor's report online, and then we went to tell her mother the news.

I share this story with you to give you a glimpse into the shock that a disability can have on yourself and those you love. Megan gave me permission to share her story with others through individual meetings, video presentations and speaking engagements. I have seen firsthand the affects of disability and have been able to help clients, myself and now my own daughter. Each one has a story that I could write an entire chapter about. Each story would demonstrate, first hand, how having disability income protection helped them and their families, keep their financial world turning.

Conversely, I have seen the devastating effects of disability on clients who chose not to acquire coverage for one reason or another, even though I explained at length the value of such coverage. (I will share some of these accounts in subsequent chapters).

At one point, early in my career, I had three consecutive clients that I approached about purchasing disability insurance who chose to "think about it" for a few weeks prior to making the decision. Each one had a disability occur that had they purchased a policy, would have been a qualified claim that could have saved their financial situation. They were left wishing they had acted sooner to get coverage in place. The real tragedy of these examples is that their disability now rendered them uninsurable for a period of time afterwards, making it impossible for them to be even considered for coverage. The contrast between clients who opted for the coverage when needed and those that did not is truly heartbreaking.

Why have I titled this book "The Forgotten Insurance?" I will tell you. I cannot tell you how many people and even financial advisors, that either don't know that Disability Income insurance exists, or how it works. Many know about it but think it's too much of a hassle to learn and work through to be worth talking about with their clients.

The problem with this is, how do you explain to a client why you didn't recommend they look at Disability Income insurance before they end up needing it most?

Has your agent ever asked to help you review your income protection plan?

I know an agent who had a client that he had taken care of for many years. One day, the client was in a terrible accident and ended up being hospitalized for many months. The client called his trusted advisor to his bedside one day and asked him,

"How long have I been a client of yours?"

"Several years," was the agent's response.

"Did I not follow every recommendation that you made to me on my financial goals and insurance?"

"Yes, you did." The agent started to get a sense of where the conversation was going.

"Why didn't you talk to me about Disability Insurance?" The client asked.

The agent stood silently for what seemed like an eternity. He didn't know what to say. He remembered that he hadn't brought it up because he felt it was too much of a hassle to learn about and to apply for. In addition, it wasn't going to happen to his client, who was healthy and a careful driver as well.

"Get out of my room!" Screamed the client.

He had had enough. He was now left with the aftermath of his accident and a painful recovery period as well as a loss of income for the duration of that time, which proved to be very long. In fact, it was not clear if he would be able to recover at all.

The agent was left with the remorse of being powerless to help his client. One that he had nurtured and tried to care for, only to find he had come up short in his duties.

This is a painful situation for the agent, who didn't ask the right questions as well as for his client, who was probably ignorant of the questions to ask about the "Forgotten Insurance." But how does one know how or what to ask in the first place?

The purpose of this book is to help empower you to be able to understand the impact of disability, even partial disability and the importance of getting Disability Insurance, and how you can determine what is best for your situation.

Over the years, I have had many common questions asked of me regarding Disability Insurance, as well as some that I bring up that are important, if the client doesn't ask me first. I intend to devote a portion of this book to those questions and how best you can answer them for yourself. Hopefully, after learning for yourself, the best solutions for you will be easy to determine on your own.

CHAPTER 1

What is Disability Insurance?

When I ask people what their most valuable financial asset is, many respond that it is their home, their retirement plan, or maybe even their estate. But what makes all of these things possible in the first place?

Wouldn't you agree that it is your ability to produce an income? If that is the case, doesn't it make sense to protect this income source as well as you can? The most important thing to remember is that we are talking about protecting your most valuable financial asset.

1

To illustrate this point, allow me to present an example (See figure 1 below)

Job A pays you $100,000 a year, but if you are too sick or to hurt to work, it pays $0. Job B, on the other hand, pays $98,000 a year, but if you are too sick or too hurt to work, it pays you $60,000 tax-free. If you were offered two jobs, which we will cleverly label "Job A" and "Job B," which would you take?

In sharing this example with many people, I have yet to have anyone say they would take Job A, even when I point out that it pays $2000 more a year. This is not to say that the cost of protecting their income is $2000 a year but rather to emphasize that people understand

2

the importance of protecting their income when it is explained in other than legal, complicated terms.

When you look in a dictionary or online, the definition is so impersonal that it makes sense why most people, if they even know Disability Insurance exists, wouldn't even be interested learning more about it.

Internet Search Results

DEFINITION: *Disability-Income (DI) Insurance "An insurance product that provides supplementary income in the event of an illness or accident resulting in a disability that prevents the insured from working at their regular employment."*

Doesn't sound too important or even something you need, given this definition, does it? I'm not sure why the word "Supplemental" is used. Especially since without it, you may not have any income to "Supplement" if you had a sickness or injury for any length of time.

In my case, I was still able to do my job but lost a half day here and a full day there on a regular basis. Disability Insurance did supplement the income that I was earning, but it alone would not have been enough for my family to survive financially, since I was the sole breadwinner in our family.

My wife was working part-time and mainly concerned with the raising of our two young children. In the case of my daughter, Disability Income Insurance was the thing that supplemented her husband's income, as she was unable to work with her disability. They went from a two-income generating family to a single income family, which seems to be the norm in today's society. I'm not trying to beat up on the definition from Investopedia, but merely trying to point out some of the reasons why this isn't my idea of an accurate and descriptive definition.

I prefer to define disability income insurance as,

"An income protection plan that provides tax-free income to you when you are too sick or too hurt to work."

It can include the ability to still perform the duties of your job, but just in a diminished capacity, which results in a loss of income due to the disability.

Although these sound similar, there are some important differences of which to take note. First, the name "Disability Insurance" in and of itself is misleading. When you think of being "disabled," isn't your first thought of someone in a wheelchair like the one painted on the handicapped parking space sign? We tend to picture someone who is unable to do much of anything, which is something that rarely happens and is therefore something that we don't think will ever happen to us. Although this does happen, it is actually the exception rather than the rule.

Think about people you have seen who have disability license plates. If they were really as disabled as those images manufactured in our minds eye, regarding disability, how would they manage to drive the car in the first place?

It's interesting that we don't name other types of insurance the same way we do Disability Insurance? For example, We don't call Life Insurance "Death Insurance," do we? We don't call it "Sickness and Accident Insurance, but rather Health Insurance. So why not call Disability Insurance by its rightful name, Income Protection Insurance? Great Britain got it right, since that is what they call it. Going forward, let's refer to it by its rightful name, "Income Protection Insurance."

Second, the income provided from this most valuable protection isn't just "supplemental." It may be the only source of income, if someone is unable to work because of a lingering disability. It can certainly supplement any income that is still coming in, but isn't our "supplemental income" the difference between being able to make ends meet and not? If we work hard, either overtime or by exceeding goals that are set, do we call the additional income that we receive "Supplemental?"

Nowadays, most individuals feel the effects of even a 20% loss in their income, let alone a total discontinuance of their paycheck because of the inability to work due to a sickness or injury.

"Most Americans are one paycheck away from the street."

Doesn't it make sense to protect yourself from such a potential financial crisis?

Finally, the word "prevents" seems to imply that it keeps you from working at all. Isn't a more likely scenario one in which you are able to return to work but in a limited capacity and therefore experience a loss of earned income? Sure, it prevents you from working full-time or making fulltime income, but in most cases, you aren't prevented from working at all.

Megan had an 8-hour surgery to remove her thyroid and 83 lymph nodes on the right side of her neck. The doctor said that 3 of these lymph nodes were the size of tennis balls. It's hard to imagine how a petite girl like Megan could have three tennis ball sized tumors concealed in her neck. To us it merely appeared as though she had gained a little weight.

The doctors indicated that she could experience pain in her neck for more than a year, as a result of the operation to remove the tumors from her lymphatic system. The medications make the pain bearable for her, but that doesn't mean she can function well, especially in a work environment. She indicates that she feels like a zombie and that she often sleeps for many hours during the day.

In addition, due to the compromise of her lymphatic system, the run of the mill illnesses that wouldn't be a big deal for many of us are more pronounced and longer in duration for Megan. The effects to her wellbeing and self-worth are almost as devastating as the cancer itself. The doctors told her that it would possibly be a year before she could even return to work, part-time.

If you think about it, you probably know someone who is "disabled." Maybe not totally disabled, but only partially so.

How many people do you know who have a bad back that keeps them from doing certain tasks at work?

How many business owners do you know who have battled cancer or heart conditions and struggled just to keep working and keep their business doors open? Do you have a family member that has been in a bad accident and unable to return to work full-time for an extended period?

Or worse still, how would you even know if someone had an illness or disability that prevented them from earning a viable income? Not being able to work is only one sign of a disabling illness. That is why it is also why it is referred to as the "Forgotten Insurance."

CHAPTER 2

Do I Need Disability Insurance?

 A man and his wife owned a very special goose. Every day the goose would lay a golden egg, which made the couple very rich.

"Just think," said the man's wife, "If we could have all the golden eggs that are inside the goose, we could be rich much faster."

"You're right," said her husband, "We wouldn't have to wait for the goose to lay her egg every day."

So, the couple killed the goose and cut her open, only to find that she was just like every other goose. She had no golden eggs inside of her at all, and they had no more golden eggs.

The moral of the story is:

"Excess greed results in nothing."

However, there is another moral that can be learned from this fable and that is:

"Wouldn't it be better to first protect or insure the eggs as they were laid, or rather the golden goose that laid the eggs?"

When I ask people this question, everyone agrees that it is best to insure the goose first, which is the reason why they have golden eggs to begin with.

In our example, you are the "goose" or income producer. The golden eggs are the resulting income and assets that will put food on the table today, and provide your nest egg for tomorrow. This makes perfect sense to most people, unless they are planning on retiring in the next few days.

However, there is a terrible "Disconnect" between the perceived value of protecting one's income and actually doing so. Why do so many people understand the importance of protecting this valuable financial asset and yet so few do anything about it?

Is it because we think that, although it happens to others, it won't happen to us? Maybe the chances of such a thing happening are so remote that we need not concern ourselves with it. Perhaps we just don't want to think about it?

A crystal ball would be helpful to us here. If we knew what was going to happen in advance, we could certainly make better decisions about the future.

If I could tell you that you would need disability insurance benefits and when you would need them, it would certainly make it easier to know just when to purchase the protection. But then it wouldn't be insurance, would it?

I learned many times the importance of a "Franklin T."

The Franklin T

PRO	CON

Ben Franklin's humble tool for decision-making: The T-Chart

On the "Pro" side of the chart, put all the positive results of the potential decision you are contemplating. On the "Con" side list the negative consequences of your decision.

If you apply this to a decision to purchase disability insurance coverage than you will see that your investment will be money well spent. Even if I made payments for many years, the benefit I receive in a time of crisis would more than compensate me in a short period of time, often in less than a year.

Right now, you may be asking,

"What if I never need to use the benefit? Haven't I just wasted my money?"

The better question is,

"If I get insurance protection for the things that I can afford to cover myself, (more on this later), have I wasted my money?"

I hope I never need to use my home insurance, but I am glad it is there in the event my house burns down. I certainly couldn't afford to replace that on my own. As a business owner, I get insurance to cover my equipment in my office, and even coverage against cyber-attacks. I certainly don't expect that any of these things will happen to me, but I would not want to be without them if they did.

You also need to take into account the probability of needing the insurance coverage in the first place. When I speak about my home, the chances that I will need to use the insurance coverage during my working lifetime is about one in a hundred. Approximately a one percent chance. The chances that I will need to use my auto insurance is about one in twenty-five, or a twenty-five percent chance.

Certainly, life insurance is a one hundred percent chance that you will use it, if you still have it in place at the time of death. Even Term Insurance, as expensive as it is, carries a one in fifty, or five percent chance of dying with the term coverage still in place. Why only one in fifty?

Because most people will change their coverage in some way before they use it. Would it surprise you to know that the chances you will use an income protection policy during your working lifetime are about one in four? That is a twenty-five percent chance.

Next to health insurance, it is the most used coverage of all. That doesn't mean it will be a total disability. It is more likely to be a partial disability that will be used.

In a group of four or more, the probability that one person in the group will use the benefit is more than eighty-nine percent. In fact, there is a ten times greater chance that you will use your income protection policy from a disability   than that

you will have a claim on a life insurance policy. Even with all of those statistics, you might still be asking how does all this apply to you?

There's a great website that is free to browse and is not put out by any insurance company, www.disabilitycanhappen.org

If you haven't heard of it before, I highly recommend giving it a look. There are tons of informative articles and information, as well as real life accounts of people who have lived with, and fought through disabilities. There are plenty of statistics on the chances of disability as well. What I recommend you look at is the section on "Chances of Disability."

This section allows you to add your specific information and get a better idea of what your chances are of becoming disabled and therefore needing a disability benefit.

Doesn't it make sense that if your chances of needing to use Income Protection Insurance are greater than the chances of using any other insurance that you might rethink a few of your decisions?

Isn't it just as important to consider carefully your Income Protection Insurance, as it is the other insurance coverages that you invest in? Certainly, since these three are the only assets that we protect, that can't be "easily replaced" if something happens.

But there is much more to the need for protecting your income than just the logical side of the equation. Protecting your ability to produce an income has a much stronger personal and emotional side to it than any other insurance protection.

Since so much of your time is devoted to producing the income that not only pays for your essentials and possibly even for your family, how would it impact you emotionally if that ability suddenly ceased?

This is one of the main reasons we buy life insurance, to replace the income that your family would lose. But how does it affect you if you "half-die," as in the case of a sickness or injury? These events reduce or eliminate your ability to provide income as well, especially if you are still around to observe the consequences.

The peace of mind of knowing that you and your family can maintain your standard of living, rather than trying to figure out how you are going to put bread on your table, is priceless.

Let's look at the case of health insurance. If I had to choose between keeping my health insurance or my income protection, I would choose to keep my income protection policy.

Sure, I could have huge medical bills from a medical emergency or long-term illness but as long as I had income I could manage my bills. If I had no income due to a sickness or injury, how would I even keep the health insurance that I probably needed in this situation?

No wonder medical bills are the cause of a lot of mortgage foreclosures. Surprisingly, most of those that lose their homes had health insurance in place. However, as the bills continue to mount, without an income stream, what would they choose to eliminate, the mortgage or the food on the table?

Certainly, going back to the "Job A" vs. "Job B" example puts in perspective the importance of protecting your most valuable financial asset.

Hopefully, you never need to use the coverage, but isn't it preferable to gamble on the loss of hundreds of dollars in premiums instead of thousands, maybe even millions of dollars in lost income over a working lifetime?

Not to mention the peace of mind that allows you to be more productive during your working lifetime, knowing that you are protected properly?

Sure, you could save for a disability, but how long would that last? If you saved ten percent of your income each year, you would need to spend 10 years' worth of savings in about a year to replace your income. There is something to be said for the peace of mind the right protection gives, to you and those most important to you. Especially in knowing you are protected against those risks that are highly probable and that are difficult if not impossible to predict. I know it saved my family's "financial bacon" to know that the coverage was there when I didn't need it, and that it was there when I did.

Here's a simple exercise worth doing. With a calculator, take your current yearly income and add to it any adjustments such as possible bonuses or pay raises you anticipate in the foreseeable future.

Now, take that number and multiply it by the number of years you plan on working until your retirement. What is the figure you come up with?

It may surprise you to find out that the number you came up with in the above exercise is close to, or even more than a million dollars.

You also need to consider what you could do with that money if you had it versus if you do not. You might call that the "Economic impact" or "Economic loss" to you and your family if you aren't able to work.

However, unlike death, the loss of income in this case occurs while you are still living. Would it surprise you to know that this is sometimes referred to as the "Living Death"?

Ask someone like my daughter Megan, and you will learn how much of an economic impact it can have.

CHAPTER 3

How Would Disability Effect My Family and I?

This is the part that very few of us ever see unless we have been, or know someone that has been, disabled; even partially. I have a client that I will call Joe who is a successful financial planner with a successful business and family. At first, he was a bit reluctant to get disability income insurance but after understanding the importance of the protection, and his wife's insisting that he do something about it, he got the protection that he needed. About a year later while riding his bike, he was rear-ended by a van, which caused severe injuries to one side of his body; especially to his leg.

Joe indicated to me that when the doctor told him he would be laid up for months, I was the first person he thought to call to be sure that all would be well. After the surgery, he had no mobility and was unable to put weight on his leg for months. He set up a temporary office at his home to try to continue working but that solution did not work out well.

Between his physical therapy appointment, his pain medication, which impaired his ability to think, and his inability to be mobile without the assistance of his wife, his regular income decreased substantially.

Even after getting back to work, it was months before he was back to where he was financially before the accident. Throughout that period, the tax-free income that he received from his disability income policy (that didn't have to be taken from his retirement or other savings for the future) is what made the difference, both physically and emotionally. He could focus on getting better rather than how to put food on the table.

Another book that I highly recommend is one by Stacy Lynne Zabriskie entitled, "The Lost Season."

(Available through Amazon at https://goo.gl/xL5tD4)

The main characters in the story are Stacy and her husband, Craig. The book chronicles the tragedy that happened when a waterskiing accident changed their lives forever. I had the chance to meet the Zabriskies and hear their story personally. Stacy told of the impact the accident had on Craig and how they weren't sure that he was going to even live. She spoke of how they weren't sure that he would ever come out of a coma and how they didn't know whether he would ever be able to move or speak again.

She went on to explain how they continue to work through the difficult circumstances that have arisen as a result of the accident. Craig spoke, with praise for the insurance agent who was so insistent that Craig get the disability insurance coverage for his family.

Stacy was able to stay with Craig and help him recover, instead of having to go to work to provide for the family. They both feel that this helped Craig to live, to fight through rehabilitation, and to recover as much as he had. Their agent was also grateful for the income that the couple received and felt rewarded that his persistence, in persuading Craig to purchase the coverage, paid off.

The devastating effects of experiencing a loss in income or worse, no income at all, can be crippling, even if it is only one paycheck missed. Most financial advisors recommend that families have adequate savings for three to six months to protect against unforeseen events. However, even that may not be enough to cope with the loss of the household's sole breadwinner.

More importantly, it can take years, even after recovery, to make up the ground lost during that period of hardship.

A disaster of that magnitude could have a devastating effect on a person's psyche. Imagine how you would feel if you weren't able to work or provide for yourself and your family for an extended period of time? What if you weren't even sure when, or if, you would be able to return to full time work at your top efficiency as before?

Many people report feelings of low self-esteem, helplessness and even depression as a result of a situation in which they don't feel they have control. We all need to feel that we are directing the events of our lives, that we affect our own destiny and our ability to reach the goals we have set for ourselves.

However, what if the ability to do so is suddenly taken away? What if we aren't all together sure if we will ever be able to be self-sufficient again?

Case studies show that even with the best care, such feelings can prolong recovery from a health setback. Doesn't it make sense to know that, even in such a situation, you will still be able to provide income to not only cover expenses but the additional expenses that come with treatment, so that you can focus on getting better?

Consider as well the effect of a disability on your spouse, children and significant people in your life. Your loved ones might have to "pick up the slack" financially. This would require them to work longer hours. Perhaps they would have to alter their future plans by going back to work in less than desirable circumstances.

Another client of mine who, due to the effects of pain medication, was not only prevented from working but also experienced a decrease in the ability to think clearly. The medication made him extremely drowsy, forcing him to sleep excessively in the afternoons. He could no longer spend the time with his children as in the past and began to be less and less a part of their lives. His young children miss his playing with them, helping them with homework, and being a bigger part of their lives.

How hard would it be for you to hear your spouse say?

"Dear, I know that you are having a hard time taking care of yourself right now, but someone's got to go to work to provide for the family. Do the best you can, and I will see you in 8 hours."

That would be extremely hard for you but equally as hard for your spouse. What if instead they could stay home and assist in your recovery at a time when you need them most.

The missing element in this scenario is earned income available when it is needed most. I find it ironic that the time you need income protection insurance the most is the very moment you cannot afford to purchase it.

There are still medical costs such as deductibles, copayments, coinsurance and out-of-pocket maximums that must be met, even with the best health care plans. All this doesn't even take in to account the rising costs of health insurance.

Wouldn't you agree that not being able to work and earn a living for an extended period of time only compounds the problem?

The need to warn my clients of the importance of Income Protection Insurance grows more and more every day. I find myself sharing my experience with my own disability on a daily basis with those I meet.

Unfortunately, you can't tell if someone is experiencing a devastating life experience simply by looking at them or talking with them. These types of situations are far too personal for most people to share with a stranger or even their friends.

And the reality is, most people would rather not hear about another's misfortunes in the first place. It seems we are all so busy in our daily lives that we rarely speak to our neighbors, let alone concern ourselves with what is going on in their lives.

In general, the effects of disability go largely unnoticed, except for those who have the obvious signs, a wheelchair, or cast or some other outward manifestation.

Perhaps this is why we really cannot comprehend how a long-term health condition can affect us and our family.

Do yourself a favor and talk to a friend, a loved one, a business associate that you know that either has had or is in the middle of an extended medical condition treatment. If you have a relationship with them, ask them to lunch and have them explain what happened and how it affected their daily schedule, their family, or their financial condition.

Ask how they felt about it and how it has affected them personally as it was happening or is happening now? Take the time to let them express their thoughts and feelings in a nonthreatening, non-rushed atmosphere where you can take the time to really listen for feelings as well as facts. You will find it not only helpful to you, but you will have helped someone else that may have never had the chance to really express their thoughts, feelings, emotions on this to anyone else. You will both be better for the experience.

CHAPTER 4

How long do people stay disabled?

Of all the questions I am asked regarding disability, this is by far the hardest to answer. Again, if I had a crystal ball to tell you how long you would need benefits, it would make my job much simpler, as well as make your decision so much easier.

A lot depends upon not only what the medical condition is to heal from, but the length of recovery time after healing. The recovery time alone can be different from one person to another as well. Megan is a perfect example of this. After her surgery, she was in the hospital for a few days and then back home to finish healing.

The healing period for Thyroid Cancer is 3 to 4 weeks but can be much longer. As of the writing of this book, Megan is still not ready to come back to work, even though it has been 10 months since her surgery.

Megan underwent an 8-hour surgery in which the doctors removed her thyroid and 83 lymph nodes. She is also enduring radioactive iodine treatment to rid her body of the remaining cancer. Even with all of these procedures, the physicians indicate that there are still more areas of cancer and that they are unsure if continued treatment will do more harm than good.

Yet the cancer, the pain, and the effects of a severely compromised immune system continue to make it impossible for her to return to normal life with her family and her profession.

As an entrepreneur, I had the attitude that is all too common. I felt that if anything happened, I could just fight through it and still be able to work. As long as I could still think, I could still do my job. That was my belief, which others shared with me as well.

Unfortunately, that theory doesn't always translate to real life. In coping with Meneire's Disease, I was first put on a medication to lessen the effects of the disease. What it did was make me feel loopy and clouded my ability to think, so much so that I was having a difficult time just keeping a clear thought or concept in my mind. Helping my clients understand fundamental concepts was beyond my ability.

I have a friend who finally cared enough about me that they confronted me and said,

"Whatever you are doing or taking, it's just not working."

That concept hadn't occurred to me. In my medicated state, I couldn't even comprehend that I wasn't able to function at the same performance level as I had before. It took my friend confronting me to bring me to a realization of my inability to do so.

Although it didn't happen instantly, I did finally find treatments that worked better, and even they had to be refined over time before I could function very well at all. In the meantime, I had lost a lot of ground. I spent a lot of time learning how to control my condition and still function on a day to day basis. Eventually I was able to regain the level of functionality I had previously. I was again able to provide for my family as I had before. For me, this process was over 5 years.

Takes Average Person up to 5 Years

My situation was by no means unique. Studies have shown that the average time required for someone to return to full work status, after suffering a debilitating accident or illness, is a little over 5 years.

This doesn't mean that I was unable to work at all for over 5 years. Quite the contrary, I was never totally disabled and not able to work. But losing a half a day here and a full day there does take its toll after a while. Many professions, like mine, build on momentum and in giving that little extra attention to clients that others may not.

I often found that taking the time to make that last phone call, or to visit that last client at the end of the day, made all the difference in my success.

That becomes extremely difficult to do, however, if you are suffering the effects of a disability. In my case, it was the onset of an "Attack" as I called it. This attack would take the form of extreme vertigo and when it occurred it would last anywhere from 30 seconds to thirty minutes.

That does not include the time it took to recover from these vertigo attacks. They left me feeling weak and unbalanced for long periods of time following the attack.

It was much like getting off of a whirling amusement park ride and trying to regain your feeling of normalcy. For me it was very difficult.

That doesn't even count the time lost to trying to bring myself back to normal after the vertigo and unbalanced feeling that I had afterwards for long periods of time. It was kind of like getting on an amusement park ride that goes in circles, and then trying to go about normal activities anytime soon afterwards. For me, it just didn't work out.

There are obviously many disabilities and recoveries that take less than 5 years, and others that take much longer. So how do you decide what the best amount of time is to have a benefit pay for? Since no one can answer that question definitively, wouldn't it make the most sense to plan for a benefit period that will provide for the longest period of time that you can afford?

This doesn't mean that you have to get the longest benefit period available, but it does mean that you should plan and obtain the best coverage available to protect your most valuable financial asset.

One key point to remember is that recovery may never fully happen. I still have attacks of vertigo, even after many years of learning how to manage them. I still have limitations that if I ignore I pay the consequences.

Because of Megan's compromised immune system, she tends to have more sicknesses and a longer recovery period as compared to the average person with a full lymphatic system. It's like a footprint: You can remove the shoe from the sand, but that doesn't mean that the effect of the shoe doesn't remain in the sand for a long time. A lot of that time can depend upon how hard and long the shoe was put into the sand, does it not?

CHAPTER 5

How do you define disability?

At this point, hopefully we can see that disabilities can and do happen. They can happen to any of us at any time. Also that there are life changing effects from someone in your family experiencing a long-term medical condition, either by sickness or injury.

But how does one define what a disability is? More importantly, how does the insurance company define a disability? After all, if the insurance company doesn't acknowledge your disability you don't receive any money. That would render your income protection policy useless.

It's obviously not as easy to define disability for an income protection policy, as it is to define death for a life insurance policy. With life insurance, either you have died, (without it being a possible exclusion of the cause of death in the policy), or you aren't dead. Even with health insurance, either you have an illness or injury that needs to be treated, or you don't.   With a disability, it isn't quite that simple.

That's why there are almost as many definitions of disability as there are insurance companies that actually provide Disability Income Insurance. A sickness or injury that one company would pay you thousands of dollars in benefits for, another company may not even consider a disability. I have seen many examples of this with clients and others. Many have been able to continue to receive a monthly income, while others have been denied for almost the same condition.

To illustrate the significant differences that these definitions can make, I would like to introduce Joe.

Joe is a successful CPA with his own thriving practice, two associate CPA's, and a staff of six employees. Joe enjoys helping others by solving their tax and accounting needs. When he retires from his practice and ultimately sells his business, he plans on pursuing his second love, which is social media. Joe has always been interested in developing and maintaining his company's social media presence, and has decided that he could use the skills that he has developed as a Social Media Strategist.

So, let's see how these definitions of disability would apply to, as well as which definition might be best for, his situation. As we review these with Joe, you might gain some insight as to which might be best for your specific situation.

There are two types of disability that we will be talking about. The first is total disability where there are three main definitions. The other type is called partial, proportionate, or residual disability. At this point, I am going to dig deeper into what these definitions are and how they apply to Joe.

The first definition of total disability is what is referred to as:

True Own Occupation. This type is defined as being unable to do the substantial and material duties of your occupation due to a sickness or injury, even if gainfully employed in another occupation.

This definition for total disability is especially important for an occupation that is highly specialized or requires a lot of education, training and experience.

If you have just spent thousands of dollars and countless hours of study, internships and work putting yourself through medical school only to find yourself unable to work due to a disability.

The last thing you would want to hear from your insurance provider is that although you can no longer practice medicine, you are still able to teach in your chosen specialty. Therefore, you do not qualify as totally disabled and are ineligible for these benefits. Not only is teaching not what you studied to do as a career, but the pay probably wouldn't be enough to cover your student loans, let alone provide for you and your family at the same level of income as you had planned.

On the other hand, if you wanted to and could do something besides be a couch potato, you could without being penalized for doing so.

Note: *the definition indicates that you will be considered totally disabled and therefore collect a full benefit, even if you are gainfully employed doing something else.*

Insurance companies can go even further with this definition to make it specific to your sub-classification specialty, as opposed to a broad category such as the license that you hold.

For example, a medical doctor could specialize in Pediatric Surgery and his insurance benefit would be specific to not being able to do this, rather than just not being able to be a doctor. A pediatric dentist could have this be their specific **"Own occupation"** definition as well.

For Joe, since he has devoted a significant amount of time and study to honing his skills as an accountant, this would be a good definition for **"Total disability"**. It means that he is not required to do something else just because of his education, training and skills. It also means that, if he wasn't able to perform the specific duties of his occupation, he could pursue his second love in Social Media without being penalized for doing so.

An important note: When we speak of True Own Occupation with Individual Disability Income Protection, it isn't the same definition as when we use the term True Own Occupation with group

Long-Term Disability. In group Long-Term Disability, the following term is used for the definition of total disability:

Modified Own Occupation. The definition for this starts out the same as true own occupation, but adds a modifier at the end:

Unable to do the substantial and material duties of your occupation due to a sickness or injury, **and not gainfully employed in another occupation.**

This means that, although you are never required to work in another occupation, even if you are able to do so, if you do work in another occupation you will no longer be considered totally disabled.

As long as you can't do your regular job and are not doing any other job, you collect a full benefit. It you decide to start a new career, your benefit can be reduced or even eliminated, depending upon how well you do at the other job. This definition works well for many people that think,

"If I can't do the job that I like or want to do, then I won't work at all."

Also, those who understand that if they do start another career, the disability income benefit would just be there to help them remain whole and not to allow them to make more than they did originally.

We will talk more about some of the differences with group long-term disability in another section. Suffice it to say that I haven't seen a group policy that has an actual true own occupation definition without the modifier of not working in another occupation at the end.

When I met Joe, our CPA, he had a good group disability policy for himself and his employees. It surprised Joe to learn that what his policy called an **"Own Occupation"** definition, didn't mean that he could do something else and still get a full benefit from his group policy.

We also discussed this third and final definition of total disability, and how it applied to his group disability income benefits:

The third definition of total disability is Any Occupation. This is defined as the inability to work in any gainful occupation for which you are reasonably suited, considering your education, training, and experience.

In other words, if you could work in another occupation that you were qualified for and could be expected to make 60% of what you made before the sickness or injury, you would be denied total disability benefits.

The job that you are qualified to do may not be what you want to do. The job may not even be available in your location. However, if you qualify for it due to your education, training and experience, it doesn't matter. This is the least favorable definition but may be the only definition that is available for unskilled jobs, where turnover is high and doing something different may not be a hardship.

One final point to consider in your individual or group disability policy is whether there is a Limited Own Occupation clause. For example, the "Own Occupation" definition is only for the first 24 months after which it then reverts to an "Any Occupation" definition.

Such a clause would be far better to discover prior to purchasing the coverage, instead of when you actually need the benefit. When we were reviewing Joe's group policy, we found that his definition had just such a clause, a 24 month of "Own Occupation," followed by an "Any Occupation" definition for the duration of the benefit.

He expressed he felt this definition would work well for his employees, but wasn't the definition he wanted for he and his associate CPA's. Joe was happy to know that there were other group policy definitions that could give him not only a better group policy total disability definition, but also supplement it with a "true own occupation" individual benefit.

Residual or Proportionate Disability is the second type of disability. This is defined as you are still working, but can't do some of the substantial and material duties of your occupation due to sickness or injury. Alternatively, you can still do all the duties of your occupation but only on a modified basis—such as part-time. In many cases, this definition also requires a loss of income due to the sickness or injury, such as 20% or more.

The benefit received would therefore be based on the percentage of lost income. So, if your income is down by 50%, you would receive half of the total disability benefit. If your income is down 66%, you would receive two thirds or 66% and so forth. This percentage can even vary from month to month depending upon the amount of income received each month until recovery.

The second type of disability, **Residual**, is something that I insist that a client have with their disability income policy. **Residual** is the more common type of disability and therefore more beneficiaries are paid under this type of partial disability than total. So, why would anyone not want that to be covered as well? There are two more points that are important to review in a disability income policy:

First, is there a period of time that I have to be totally disabled before I can collect on a residual disability benefit? This type of waiting clause makes the policy harder for the insured individual to collect, and as such would lower the premium, much like a high deductible for other types of insurance.

Second, does the residual definition say that I have to have a loss of time and duties as well as a loss of income, or does it say that I only have to meet one of the three?

The more liberal the definition here, the more chance that a benefit will be paid and not denied. This can make the difference of thousands of dollars of benefits to you and your family.

There are hundreds of subtle nuances in these definitions, therefore, getting the right information from an experienced professional in each of these types of coverage can be vital in your search for the best policy. As with Joe in our example above, making the right choices in your insurance policy can make the difference to the tune of thousands of dollars and could be tens of thousands over the course of his working lifetime.

For the seven years that I received disability income benefits, it made thousands of dollars of difference to me and to my family.

As you can imagine, the discussion I had with Joe as to his perception of the disability benefits, and the reality of what his disability benefits actually were became invaluable to him. Joe's perception of his group benefits versus the real situation is not uncommon. In fact, many of my clients have the same misconceptions when we first meet.

CHAPTER 6

What types of disabilities will a policy pay for?

Many people that I talk to initially believe that income protection is just in case of an injury or accident from which they will take a long time to recover from or that cripples them for life. Although these types of accidents occur, they only account for about 10% of all claims for disability income.

I have a client who is a dentist. He wasn't sure he needed an income protection policy because he did not believe he would ever be disabled to the point of not being able to work.

We had a discussion regarding the most common types of sickness or injury, especially those that do not keep you from being able to perform your duties at work. Instead, they limit your ability to work as long as necessary or as effectively as before.

He had not considered that and afterward decided to get the protection that he and his family needed. Two years later, he developed a back condition. He wasn't able to find relief from the medical or the chiropractic community. Although he could still work after only 4 hours, the pain was so intense that he would need to be flat on his back for the rest of the day. His ability to work was cut in half and his income dropped proportionately soon thereafter.

I helped him file his disability claim and he was happy to receive a tax-free benefit for 50% of the total benefit. I still check to see how he is doing. He and his family are grateful he decided to get this most vital coverage, even though he thought he would never use it.

Right now, you are probably wondering, what other types of disabilities does income protection cover? Rather than boring you with the dry statistics, let's play a game similar to "Family Feud."

Let's pretend you are one of the contestants trying to give me the top 5 answers on the board to the following question:

Name the top 5 claims by category for disability income benefits.

Name the top 5 claims by category for disability income benefits.

Your hand shoots up as you hop up and down excitedly.

As you are selected to respond you shout enthusiastically,

"Accidents or Injuries!"

The host looks to the board and says,

"Show me Accidents or Injuries!"

You hear that welcome ding as the third slot rotates to reveal your correct answer. Incidentally, this category represents 10.3% of all claims according to one major insurance company.

The host continues,

Congratulations, that is the #3 most popular answer. These are definitely events that can change our lives and financial situations dramatically. An associate of mine, who enjoyed taking time off from his financial practice during the winter months to teach skiing, found out all too tragically how this can happen. In trying to demonstrate to his class some things that you shouldn't do when skiing; he was hospitalized with major injuries, which he still suffers from to this day. Now back to the game.

Again, you raise your hand and hop like a joyful rabbit.

The host selects you again and you say,

"How about Mental and Nervous Conditions?"

Turning to the board the host proclaims,

"Show me Mental and Nervous Conditions!"

Once again, you hear the rewarding ding and another panel rotates to reveal your answer.

"Excellent", says the Host. "You gave us the **#4 response** from our polling audience. This category represents 9.1% of all insurance claims."

The host continues,

"Okay, this a follow up to the last question. if you are too anxious or too depressed to work, even if only part-time, would that have an effect on your ability to earn an income or even to recover? Be careful with this one, since many disability income policies limit benefits for this to 2 years LIFETIME.

You pause to contemplate the question and then cheerfully respond,

"Of Course!"

"That is correct", says the host. "Okay, we have the #3 and the #4 answers on the board. Who wants to try for the #1 answer?"

You shoot up your hand again and the host gives you a weary smile and says,

"Okay, what is your answer?"

Of course, you have studied this book prior to playing the game and you remember Megan and her touching experience fighting cancer so you shout out,

"Cancer!"

"Show us Cancer!" bellows the host.

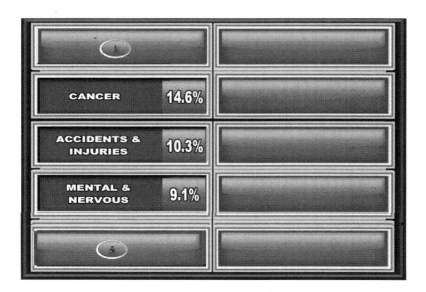

Ding, ding, ding goes the board and the #2 slot rotates to reveal your selected Answer.

"Great, that is the #2 answer based on our survey. This category represents 14.6% of the insurance company surveyed' claims. Not too long ago, this category was in the 5th position, but has climbed to the 2nd most common disability claim. We all know someone who has or has had to deal with cancer and its treatment. With the exception of maybe non-malignant skin cancer, this can change anyone's life in the blink of an eye.

"Okay, there are only two answers left on the board. You need to answer both to win. What is your guess?"

You pause to think and recall that Greg told you his story about his experience with Meneire's Disease. But that can't be the category, it is only one of many in that category. You recall Googling the definition of Meneire's Disease where it listed it as a Neurological Disease, although that was just a guess as to the cause since it is still unknown.

You excitedly begin jumping up and down again,

"How about Neurological Disease!"

"Show me Neurological Disease!" Proclaims the host.

Buzzzzzz, an annoying buzzer sounds signaling an incorrect answer and a bit red X appears next to the board, the first of three you are allowed.

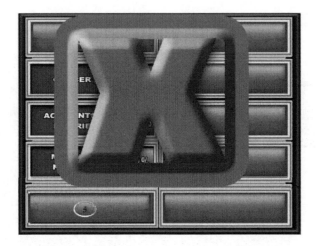

The host says,

"Oohh, so sorry. That's not on the board and that's you first strike but you still have two more chances. Neurological disease is actually #6, representing 6.9% of all claims. Neurological Disease is tough to diagnose, tough to treat and tough to recover from. The challenging part is that many the cause of many of these are unknown as is the related recovery time.

Your brow furrows as you concentrate. Then it hits you. Your friend just had a baby. But that's not a disability, you think to yourself. Suddenly you remember an article you read that indicated that maternity can be considered a disability, especially when the doctor requires you to be restricted to bed rest for the duration of the pregnancy due to toxemia or elevated blood pressure. The article went on to include other maternity complications such as Placenta Previa and C Section deliveries. You smile and say,

"Maternity!"

The host gives you a doubting look but says,

"Show me Maternity!"

Again, you hear the annoying buzzer indicating your second wrong answer.

"Oh, tough luck. Maternity is not on the board. One wrong answer left, think carefully. Maternity is actually #7, if the board went that high. It represents 5.1% of all disability claims.

Small beads of sweat begin to form on your brow as you concentrate even harder. Your mind recalls a close friend who runs daily, eats right, and watches his weight, and yet had an unexpected heart attack that almost took his life. If he hadn't decided to go to the hospital when he felt some pain in his chest, he probably wouldn't have made it. It took him months to recover and be released from the doctor's care.

Cautiously you look at the host and say, in a less than confident voice,

"Cardiovascular Disease?"

"Show me Cardiovascular Disease", trumps the host.

You experience a burst of relief as the familiar ding sounds, signaling your correct answer. On the board the #5 answer panel rolls over. You hear the host say,

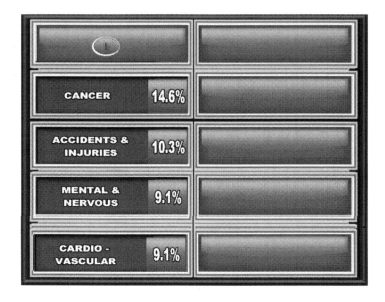

CANCER 14.6%	
ACCIDENTS & INJURIES 10.3%	
MENTAL & NERVOUS 9.1%	
CARDIO - VASCULAR 9.1%	

"Correct! Great job. Cardiovascular Disease is actually tied with the #4 answer, Mental and Nervous Conditions. However it is our #5 category and It also results in 9.1% of all claims."

You take a moment to ponder your surprise that this condition isn't higher on the board. You are yanked from your reflections by the host who says,

"Okay, you're still in the game but you still have one unanswered panel to worry about. What is your answer?"

Just a note here: When I have played this game with clients, I find that the #1 answer is the toughest one for them to get. This is one area that doesn't seem to be a respecter of how well one takes care of themselves either, and can be anywhere from annoying to totally debilitating. Dentists, Chiropractors, Construction Workers, People behind a computer and just about any other profession can have trouble in this area. Now back to the game.

You again concentrate. Now your shirt is beginning to show signs of perspiration as you dab a handkerchief on your forehead.

What could the #1 Answer be? You think to yourself as you grab your neck, then it hits you. You remember your recent bout with back pain and shout,

"Back trouble! I mean, Musculoskeletal Disorders!"

"Show us Musculoskeletal Disorders", booms the host.

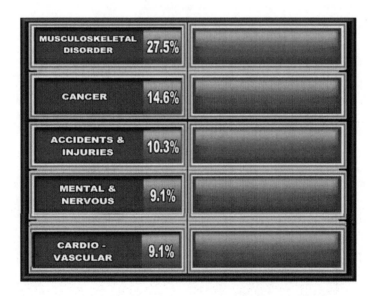

Whew, there it is, the pleasing dinging bell signaling your correct answer. You look with joy as you see the top panel rotate to reveal your selection.

"The #1 answer", bellows the host. "Congratulations! You guessed the #1 answer. Musculoskeletal Disorders account for 27.5% of all claims. Remember, this isn't just back pain, slipped or degenerative discs. There are 200 disorders of the connective tissue alone that range from something you can live with to something you would rather live without."

So there you have the top five, (Seven if you count the two additional categories) disability categories. One out of four adults, 20 years or older, entering the workforce today will be disabled before age 65. Every 12 seconds someone is disabled. Over 12% of the US population is disabled with half of those between ages 18 and 64. These are real people that will all tell you that getting disability income protection is one of the smartest things that you can do.

The obvious disabilities that are not paid for would be self-inflicted injuries and an injury that was sustained while committing a felony. So don't rob a bank and get shot as you leave. If you do, don't expect to collect a disability income benefit, (like you would get the urge to do so in the first place). You should check the limitations and exclusions for any other disability categories that might be included.

Although my dentist client was in the top category for claims, even he didn't believe that he would ever need to use his coverage.

Most people don't. By purchasing disability insurance, you are taking a chance of making a small financial mistake.

However, isn't that preferable to making a much larger financial mistake when the time comes that you actually need the benefit and don't have it?

CHAPTER 7

How does a disability income policy pay me?

This is a question that I am asked almost every time I meet with someone new. When I was talking to a referral from one of my closest clients, whom I will call John.

He initially said he wasn't interested in disability income protection because he didn't believe that it would every actually pay any benefit to him but rather to his doctors or hospital, similar to health insurance.

"That's what I have health insurance and worker's compensation for, "he added. He was surprised at my response.

I told John that most disability income policies pay on an "indemnification" basis. This basically means that the policy will pay you a monthly amount, (depending upon whether it is total or residual), after a specified waiting or elimination period.

"Sounds simple enough, but is there more to it than just that?" he asked.

We then spent some time discussing the points that were most important to him and his specific situation:

Actually, there is a lot more to it than just that. There are a few different things that you need to know to determine how you receive this pay out:

First, how did you pay for the premium of the policy? If you pay the premium with pre-tax dollars, or if your company pays the premium for you, then the benefit is taxable. If you pay for the premium with after-tax dollars and don't take a deduction for the premium, (which many times is not even possible to do), then the benefit is paid tax-free. The IRS basically says you can pay them now or pay them later.

Personally, I would rather pay the little bit of tax on the premium as opposed to the bigger amount of tax on the entire benefit, wouldn't you?

Let's say I have a "60% of income" benefit policy through my work, which is paid for by the company. It's great that there is no cost to me. Sure, it might feel a little tight at 60% of my gross income but I could probably get by, right?

Well, the first thing that you need to remember is that the benefit paid out is taxable. That just turned your 60% benefit into much less money, possibly as low as 45% of your income, depending on the amount that needs to be taken out for Federal and State income taxes.

To make matters worse, during the first 6 months, the Federal Government says that you have to pay FICA taxes on that income, which takes out another 7.65% or so. Even more if you are the boss and responsible for the other half of the FICA portion required by the IRS as a matching amount.

Finally, you need to remember that, if you are on disability claim from work and your health insurance is being partially paid for by your employer, you will probably be approached by them to let you know that you can keep your health insurance with the following caveat. Since you are not working full-time, you need to pay the full amount of the premium each month in order to keep it in force.

Again, isn't it ironic that when you need it most, it will probably be the least affordable option for you? Now how much of your income are you left with? Try doing the math—the answer will surprise you.

You also need to know your definition of income that is used in the policy to determine how the policy will pay you. If your income consists of more than just salary or hourly income, say bonuses, overtime, dividends, owner profits and other such items, but your policy only covers your salary or hourly income, you may be surprised how little of your income is really covered and how low a % of benefit you will receive.

In some instances, I have seen policies that only pay for a total disability and only a flat amount payout for a limited period of time. The time old adage that "you get what you pay for" was never more applicable than it is with income protection.

These are all things that you need to consider when reviewing this most important area of protection. We will discuss more on "What do I do now?" in another section.

CHAPTER 8

What should I look for in a disability policy?

If you are like most people I meet with, even if you have disability income protection, you probably have not read through the policy to know exactly what it does and does not cover. So many times, there is a perception that there is a certain level of coverage and protection, but when you investigate what the benefit actually is, it is quite different.

If you look at a real disability policy, it can be more than 100 pages of text.

These documents intended to be legal documents and have been challenged in court on specific language and specific situations countless times. So, unless you are an attorney interested in reading and understanding every detail, how do you know what to look for?

Nowadays, disability income policies are required to have a Summary of Benefits, which you can refer to. Similar to a Summary of Benefits for Health Insurance, this is an abbreviated version of the real policy, summarizing some of the key benefits and definitions. No two companies have the same definitions and benefits. One company may want to emphasize a particular benefit that others don't have, while another company may have a different benefit that is unique to them. So how do you know which is best for you and your needs?

Before considering the definitions and benefits, you need to ask yourself 3 important questions:

1) How long do I want to wait for the company to pay a benefit after I am either 'totally' or 'residually' disabled? This is called the waiting/elimination Period.

2) How much benefit do you want the insurance company to pay to you after the waiting period? This is known as the total benefit amount.

3) How long do you want the benefit amount to be paid? Known as the maximum benefit period.

Since you are protecting your most valuable financial asset that makes all of your other assets and their protection possible, you should strive for the longest period of time that you can get, right? Then, depending on your specific situation and needs, you can customize these options to fit what works best for you.

If you were to search the internet for the most important points to look for in a disability income policy, you would find some common areas of agreement among the specialists in the field. Although there is some discussion as to the importance of some of these even among so called "experts," there are some important things to consider in a disability policy, such as:

Is the policy both guaranteed renewable and non-cancellable?

The first provision (guaranteed renewable) means that you (or your company) can keep the policy as long as you want to pay for it. The second part (non-cancellable) means that the company cannot change the benefits or the premium for the life of the policy, unless you want to make a change to it yourself.

Why is this an important definition to understand?

Because you need to understand how much of the risk in a policy you want the insurance company to take, while guaranteeing that the premium and benefit can or cannot change during the time that you own the policy;

What is the definition of total disability?

In a previous chapter, we discussed the different definitions, and which might apply best for different types of professions. Some would argue that **"True Own Occupation"** is the only acceptable definition to purchase.

There is no absolute answer here. It all depends on what is best for you and your situation. For someone like Joe, our CPA with a specialized practice, a **"True Own Occupation"** definition could be important. For someone that could easily transition to another job if unable to do their current occupation due to sickness or injury, a **"Modified Own Occupation,"** or possibly even an **"Any Occupation"** definition might be adequate;

What is the definition of residual disability?

We discussed these provisions and differences as well. Is the definition a loss of time or duties and a loss of income, or is it just a loss of income due to sickness or injury?

It could even be an **"OR"** definition where you only need a 20% loss of time or of duties, or income. The differences can make thousands of dollars of benefit difference at claim time, so consider it carefully. Please review this most important discussion on this definition from **Chapter 5**, and consider how it applied to Joe, as well as to your own specific situation and occupation;

What is the definition of income?

Please refer to Chapter 7 for the answer to this question, where it was discussed in detail.

What is the maximum benefit for total disability?

The policy may say it will pay a benefit of covered income but the maximum benefit available may be much less than 60% of your income, because your income far exceeds the "covered amount." You don't want to learn about that surprise the hard way, when you need the benefit!

I have a friend that was sure his group disability benefit would be fine until one day when he was diagnosed with MS. Like many disabilities, it wasn't considered a total disability at first, but gradually became worse. Only at this point did he finally realize that his group policies had a maximum benefit "cap" of $5000 per month of benefit that would be paid. This ended up being only about a third of what his actual earnings were previously.

Is my disability income benefits offset by other personal and social disability programs? In other words, will my benefits be reduced if I qualify for worker's compensation, Social Security

Disability benefits, and profit sharing from my company, or even by another disability policy that I have?

These public or social benefits reduce your benefit, dollar for dollar, if you qualify for them. In many cases, a group disability policy may require you to make application for these benefits, which will then minimize the amount that the company will be required to pay you at the time you need it most.

What other benefits come with or are available with the policy?

There are some additional benefits that come with a policy, such as the premium being waived while you are on claim. You can also get an additional benefit for rehabilitation, since that is in your best interest, as well as the insurance company's.

As far as others benefits available, ask yourself these questions.

Do you want the benefit to increase each year that you are on claim to keep up with inflation? (Cost of Living Benefit)

Do you want a greater benefit if you have something catastrophic happen to you, such as Alzheimer's or if you are paralyzed? (Catastrophic Disability Benefit)

Is it important to get your premiums refunded to you at retirement if you don't ever use the benefit? (Premium Refund Option)

There are many more options depending upon the company issuing the policy but these are a few of the main points to carefully consider.

It's a good idea to look at more than one insurance company and get a better idea of the differences in benefits and options each offers. Since you will want to look at more than one company, it's also a good idea to work with an agent that deals with many different insurance companies, so that you can get a more unbiased opinion.

You will find that some companies work wonderfully for specific professions but are not as good with definitions and benefits when dealing with other professions. Still others may be looking at a particular target market of professions. Just like your clothing, there is no "one size fits all." Option. However, unlike clothing, it's the detail in the 100 plus page document that will hurt you, even more than the size of a garment.

CHAPTER 9

Is Disability Income Protection Expensive?

This is a great question. One that I am asked quite often in dealing with clients. Suppose you went to the auto dealer and when you first met a salesperson, you asked them,

"How much is it to buy a car?"

The dealer would probably ask you what you would like your vehicle to do, whether it was for business or personal use, what features you would like, and what make and model are you interested in.

How would the dealer be able to answer the question without first gathering some information? If they did answer with a price, wouldn't you want to know what you were getting for the amount that they were quoting you?

The better question to ask is,

What is the potential benefit that I will receive to protect against my risk, and is it worth the premium that I will be paying for it?

I have yet to have someone ask me the question this way, so let me explain why this is the better question.

"Expensive" is a relative term and depends upon your income. If you make $50,000 a year, then a $10,000 premium would be 20% of your income, and would probably be considered expensive. On the other hand, if your income were $1,000,000 a year, then a $10,000 premium would be 1% of your income and probably not be considered expensive.

In addition, expensive depends upon the perceived value of what it is you are considering.

Let's revisit our earlier example of the "Job A" vs. "Job B" diagram. If the premium to protect my $100,000 of annual income was 2% or $2000 for $60,000 a year of tax-free benefit, I have yet to have someone say that it isn't a good value for the protection and therefore not expensive.

Finally, I need to consider the potential payout of the benefit for the premium that I am paying. A recent client of mine who was a bit older was looking at a policy available to him that would pay $6500 a month of benefit, with both total and residual benefit and a cost of living increase benefit of $400 a month.

He considered that to be rather expensive. When we looked at it in more detail, we saw that the company was ready to pay over to him $2,000,000 worth of benefit tax-free if he were disabled for 20 years for about $13 a day, with a premium that was guaranteed not to go up, (non-cancellable).

We decided that, for the amount of benefit that would be paid tax-free to protect his most valuable financial asset, this was a good investment in himself and his protecting his ability to produce an income for him and his family.

This isn't to suggest that a policy needs to be that much to be good. Ideally, we want to protect our "asset" the best we can. For this individual, we looked at several options and decided that this was best. It is important for you to answer the 3 questions mentioned earlier,

How long of waiting period do I want?

How much benefit do I want or need?

How long do I want to have that benefit pay?

These questions offer many combinations and there are different insurance companies that you can review to help you determine what the best combination is for you and your specific needs.

You can even work backwards with a specific budgeted amount. You can find the best combination of options offered by a company that will yield the most benefit and best definitions for you and your budget. You can then review this each year to be sure that it is still what is best for you and your needs.

There are little known options that are especially good for a professional who is just starting their career and needs a good benefit to cover personal expenses that are now higher due to his new business venture. Perhaps the new business hasn't quite gotten to the level of profitability to maintain the premium needed for that benefit. How do you get the best of both worlds?

One of my clients was a recently graduated medical doctor and was facing that exact situation. He knew what he wanted and needed, but was having a difficult time with the level premium that it would take to get the benefit he had chosen.

We looked at a "Graded Premium" to solve his problem. Similar to term insurance, a Graded Premium allows you to start with a lower amount at the beginning (as much as 40% less or more) and increase that amount little by little each year. His strategy was to start this way, but to convert to a level premium in 2 to 3 years when his practice was mre profitable and before the premium started becoming to expensive to maintain long-term, (again, similar to term life insurance). This allowed him to get the benefit that he wanted at a premium that he could afford.

Ultimately, the most expensive disability income policy that you can purchase is the one that doesn't pay a benefit when you need it most. Disability Income Insurance is the worst policy to buy on price alone. Be sure what you purchase is for the right amount of benefit, with the right provisions and the right company. If done right, the policy will also be the right premium for you. It will make a world of difference at claim time.

I often ask those I talk with,

"Which would you rather have; $0 a month, $500 a month, or $1000 a month?"

I have yet to have anyone say they wouldn't want the $1000 a month. I have also had many ask,

"What is the catch?"

I explain to them that these are examples of benefit amounts from three different insurance companies for a specific disability claim. Once we have gone through the claim scenario with the three different plans, as many of my clients have, they almost always want the one that would pay the highest benefit. Does that make it expensive? The answer is no!

CHAPTER 10

How else can I cover my financial needs during a disability?

I still remember talking with one gentleman that, after we had reviewed the options for protecting his income best, finally determined that he would pass on getting any protection. He felt he had the financial resources to cover any disability that might occur. I asked what type of resources he had for such a financial crisis. He indicated that he had saved 10% of his income over the past 20 years and it would be enough to get by.

When we did the math, he was surprised to see that his nest egg would only last him about two years. That didn't even take into account the penalties and taxes involved in withdrawing it from his retirement plan in the first place.

Besides disability income protection, do I have other ways that I can protect myself against the risk?

The answer is yes, but will they really work for you? Let's look at some of the options and consider how well they work.

You could self-insure.

If you have monies in savings and/or a retirement account, you could use those funds to provide the income that you need for a disability, but for how long?

Would they cover you for 6 months, a year, or more than 5 years? Is that really what you want to use those funds for? Wouldn't you be better off leveraging the resources of a good insurance company to provide you income for the time that you need it?

If you took it out of a retirement account, would you pay a penalty for early withdrawal and taxes that would further erode the amount you withdrew?

What would you do when it came time to retire? If you have used all of your savings and retirement just trying to get to retirement age.

How would you make up the lost "time value of money" for using the funds prematurely?

? Can't I just get Social Security Disability Benefits? There is a benefit available that could help but how does it work?

First, we should look at the definition of disability from Social Security viewpoint.

The law defines Disability as:

"The inability to engage in any substantial gainful activity (SGA) by reason of any medically determinable physical or mental impairment(s) which can be expected to result in death or which has lasted or can be expected to last for a continuous period of not less than 12 months."

This is a harder definition to qualify under than the "Any Occupation" definition that we looked at earlier. At least that one is based on your education, training, and experience in order to be deemed a gainful occupation for you.

It's no wonder that 65% of all Social Security disability claims are denied. Even if you do qualify, it is after a 180 day elimination period, and generally takes 6 – 12 months before you can begin to receive any benefit at all. Even when you do receive your benefits, the average is about $1200 a month or less, which would not be enough for most people to afford their mortgage, utilities and groceries. In addition to

77

initially qualifying, you need to continue to re-qualify on a regular basis. The odds are definitely against you on this one.

Why not obtain the income protection benefit that meets your specific needs, with Social Security Disability as an added benefit, if you are actually able to qualify?

 **Well, won't Workers Compensation provide income for me?**

Although this benefit is required by employers who provide for their employees, but not for employers themselves, it may not be enough for a long period of time.

First, if you are an employer, this can be very expensive coverage for you to obtain. Since you can almost say that you are "on the clock" for most of the day, the cost can far outweigh the potential benefit you could receive.

Only 5% of all disability claims are work-related. To qualify, you have to be able to prove the disability was on-the-job and that you were unable to work at all because of the injury. By the way, illnesses are very difficult to prove as being "on the job" related. Even if you do qualify for the benefit, it is a limited amount that you receive and generally only for a limited time.

The better approach in most cases, especially for a business owner, is to have a good health insurance policy and a great disability income policy that covers both on and off the job. One that covers your expenses, with any benefit that might be received from Workers Compensation as an unexpected bonus.

Why can't I just have my family take care of me?

Let's think about that one for a minute. In order to actually have this as a plan, you first need to be talking with your family on a regular basis, to be sure that they will be willing to help support you for what could be an extended period of time.

My family loves me very much, but even with five other Brothers and Sisters, they each have their own set of challenges, their own set of financial limitations, and their own family to deal with. Having to support me and possibly my wife as well would create an undue hardship on them.

Before I got into the financial services industry, I went through a period of unemployment. I had to swallow my pride and ask for financial help from my family while I was looking for a job, since unemployment was not enough. I was grateful that it was only for a couple of months, and that I then was able to pay them back for their generosity and support.

That arrangement would not have worked long term. I was more grateful that I didn't have to depend on them during my years of disability and recovery to full-time employment status. Unless you have a very rich relative that has more money than they know what to do with, this becomes a very challenging solution that would strain even the best family relationships.

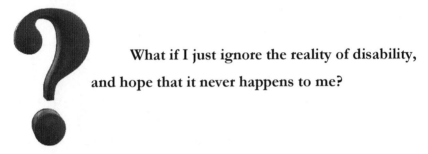

What if I just ignore the reality of disability, and hope that it never happens to me?

Which would you consider the bigger gamble in the case of my client that I referred to earlier,

To pay $400 a month for 20 years and never have used the benefit, (a $96,000 "mistake" over time), or to not have the coverage and lose $6500 month of income, plus inflation, (an over $2,000,000 mistake).

There is an immeasurable peace of mind that comes from knowing you have taken care of the three biggest risks to your future: Health, Wealth and Life.

Over the years, I have heard many other solutions that people have offered as to how they would cover this very real risk to their financial plan. I have to share with you my favorite story that I have heard over the years:

A younger couple I was speaking to about what their goals were for the future and how best we could protect them, told me that they didn't feel either of them were going to be disabled that year. They asked me to check with them the following year to see how they felt at that time. I truly didn't know how to respond to that request.

"Why don't you call me when you feel like you will need the protection?" I asked.

Hopefully, they do so before they experience a disability that makes it impossible for them to get the protection they need.

Coincidentally, a few months later, I was skimming through some television channels when I came upon an old Twilight Zone episode. The scene starts with a younger couple across the dining room table from an insurance salesman, explaining to the agent that they didn't feel like they needed life insurance.

The agent's eyes roll back as if in a trance. He proclaims that in just three weeks from that day, they will be traveling down a back road and be unable to make the turn. He goes on to explain that their car will overturn, and they will die instantly.

The couple look at each as if this guy is out of his mind and they hurry him out of the house. Three weeks later, the agent is talking to his manager and is trying to figure out why, even when he tells someone exactly what is going to happen, that they still don't purchase life insurance from him.

I was kind of hoping that the couple I referred to above had been watching this same episode, but I decided that whether I was right or they were right, it wouldn't make much difference. Especially at the time they actually needed the benefit. I hope that none of my clients ever need the benefit, just like I hope that they never need to use their home or auto insurance.

However, people are very grateful that they have the right protection when they need it. They are also grateful for the peace of mind and added productivity that they feel for protecting their most valuable asset.

Any of the things we have discussed could be a partial answer you could use to supplement the leveraged value of a good disability income policy and thus allow you to not need as much benefit, (except possibly the last one that we discussed).

However, it doesn't look like any of them are good alternatives, unless you are ready to retire tomorrow.

CHAPTER 11

What about my company's disability policy?

This one question alone could take several pages to fully answer. There are some very lively discussions between Group Benefits Disability Specialists and Individual Disability Income Specialists as to the advantages and limitations of group long-term disability benefits and individual disability income benefits.

Both group and individual disability income benefits have changed and improved over the years. The real question is:

Are my group long-term disability benefits enough?
(Assuming that I have them at all)

When I talk with employees of companies, many vaguely remember hearing something about a group disability benefit that is provided by their company. Even many company owners may not be aware of whether they have a group benefit. If they do, most don't remember the details. Far too many don't even recall if they signed up for the benefit when it was offered or not. Still, even fewer can recall the name of the insurance company it is with, or how much of a benefit they have.

As a Group Benefits Disability Specialist and a Disability Income Fellow, (a fancy name for a Group Disability Income Specialist), I have studied extensively the group long-term disability market. I have also been able to help many companies to provide this valuable benefit for themselves and their employees.

Sadly, in many cases, this is the only way that many people receive an income replace benefit at all. Although most people believe that they have some benefit available through work, almost 69% of American workers do not have an income protection benefit. It's a good idea to find out what you may actually have before relying on it too heavily to be there when you need it.

If you are fortunate enough to have such a benefit available, make sure that you are actually signed up for the benefit. If you miss your initial eligibility, you may have a difficult time getting enrolled later on. Also, get a copy of at least the "Summary of Benefits" that will describe the benefit and how it works. At this point, I would highly recommend that you hire an agent who specializes in both group and individual disability income benefits. Have them review the coverage with you, so that you understand how it works, what it takes to qualify for the benefit, the potential taxation of the benefits received, and even how much benefit will be available to you in the case of a long-term disability. Many people are surprised that the benefit is not as much as they thought it would be.

There are some key points to review in the policy, to better understand how the benefit works. They include:

 # Is the benefit taxable?

If the company pays the premium, the benefit is received by you as taxable income, (and may also be subject to FICA taxes for the first 6 months). If you pay for the premium with after-tax dollars, the benefit is tax-free. Don't assume just because you see some money coming out of your paycheck, even after taxes that this means you are paying the premium. You might only be paying a portion of the total premium, which would mean only a portion of the benefit received is tax-free.

For example, if your income is $100,000 per year, and your benefit for a total disability is $60,000, understanding the effects of this being taxable can be an eye-opening experience:

You would first deduct the 7.65% for FICA in the first 6 months, (if you are the employer, that would be double that amount that would need to be paid for this alone). Next, you deduct your Federal and State taxes from the $60,000 of benefit. You may also want to take into account any contributions to your retirement plan that you will probably not receive while on claim, as well as any other costs that you may incur, such as the employer's portion of your health insurance that you will probably need to pay, since you are no longer working full time.

? What amount of "spendable" income to come up with?

You may find that the number is more like 35-40% of your pre-disability earnings, rather than the 60% you would have if the benefit were tax-free. Is it worth the small deduction in the premium to pay more on your benefit when need most?

If I pay for the benefit, do my premiums go up over time?

Most group long-term disability policy premiums go up in two ways:

First, they usually go up as you get older. This can be an increase each year or in 5-year increments, or even longer. Not only do the premiums get much higher as you approach 65, (since the chances of being out on disability increase), but the benefit period reduces then as well.

Second, the insurance company can increase the overall premiums to your company on an annual basis at "renewal" of the policy. One key here is to be sure that you are working with a strong insurance company that has a good history of keeping premiums stable, and who will be there when you need them.

What is the pre-existing condition clause in the policy?

Most group disability policies can be obtained without medical questions or financial documentation required. But there is a provision that protects the insurance company with this. The pre-existing condition clause usually indicates a period of time that the company can look back from when the coverage went into effect. They are checking to see if there were any medical conditions that you were treated for or had consultation on. They also will check to find out if you took prescriptions, had surgery or hospitalization, etc. Their search is to discover anything that can be termed pre-existing. These can even include a condition that a reasonable person would have sought treatment for, but that you didn't. This can get a bit sticky at claim time.

I had a client that obtained life insurance coverage but felt he was fine when he enrolled in his company's group disability income policy, and turned down an individual policy to supplement his group coverage. 3 months later, he went to the doctor to find out about a nagging headache that he had for a while. The headache turned out to be a brain tumor. When he tried to make a claim, he was told that it was considered to be a pre-existing condition. The reasoning was that since he had the headache for some time and a reasonable person would have seen a doctor for the condition that he should have known about the problem. How do you fight the doctor's notes of what the history is for such an event?

Thus, if there is something that qualifies as pre-existing under these provisions, the policy will not pay a benefit for a disability that is a cause of, or contributed to by this condition that happens for a period of time after the coverage goes into effect. Some policies provide a limited benefit during this period of time, so be sure that you know how your policy reads on this crucial point. This would have helped my client tremendously with the financial burden of this tragedy, if it had been available to him.

What is the definition of income? As discussed before, if the definition only includes salary or regular hourly wages, it does not cover overtime, bonuses, dividends, K-1 income, owner profits, employer contributions to your retirement plans, etc. Many business owners and employees rely on these types of earned income as much as their regular income. How much of your income may not be covered under such a definition? It is worth the time to figure this one out.

? How often is my benefit updated to keep up with my rising income?

This is one point that many companies forget to update. Each year, as incomes increase, your company should report changes in employees' income to the insurance company, so that you are covered for the correct amount of income, and thus the correct amount of benefit.

I have asked several companies how often they update the income of their employees to the insurance company, only to find that they haven't done so in years. The insurance company will only pay up to the amount of income that is being protected by the policy, whether group or individual. This can definitely affect the amount of benefit that business owners and their employees will receive if this hasn't been updated regularly.

? What are the definitions of total and residual disability?

This is important to know so that you know what it takes to qualify for a benefit from the policy. We have reviewed these definitions in a previous section so I won't go into the detail again. Be careful to note if the initial definition changes to a different definition of disability after a period of time. This can mean the difference between receiving income for the entire duration of your medical condition and recovery, rather than finding out that the insurance company has determined you can do something else and terminates your claim.

How long is the elimination period before benefits can be received, and how is it met?

Is the waiting period a period of total disability before you can qualify, or can partial/residual disability help to meet it? Is it a loss of time or duties, plus a % of income that is lost before you can satisfy the waiting period? Is it a continuous period of time to meet the waiting period, or can there be a period of trying to go back to work and then realizing that it isn't going too well without starting the waiting period over? How long can you go without a paycheck? These are all questions that an experienced specialist can help you answer in your review of your coverage.

How long is the benefit period for receiving benefits?

Will the benefit only be for 6 months? 2 years? 5 years? To Social Security Normal Retirement Age (SSNRA)? Many people that I talk to are surprised to learn how little time their income will be paid by their group policy. Would you rather know before or after you need the benefit?

What potential benefits may reduce my benefit amount?

These are often called "offsets," which reduce your benefit when you receive them. Examples would be Workers Compensation received, Social Security Disability Benefits, and settlements from an auto accident claim. Others include sick pay, and even potentially individual disability income benefits that you own personally. As we discussed previously, many people are surprised to find out how many things will reduce their benefit that they are counting on receiving.

Are there any other benefits or limitations?

Besides the fact that your employer actually owns the policy and therefore can decide to change companies or drop the coverage altogether at their discretion, there may be some other limitations. These could include:

No Cost of Living Adjustment benefit. Mandatory rehabilitation to have benefits continue or even requiring you to make application for Social Security, Workers Compensation, or other benefits to see if you qualify as means of determining the offset to your benefit.

There are many different definitions and benefits, even with the same insurance company. Therefore, it's a great idea to have someone with experience in the industry who works with many businesses review these critical components of your group benefits. They can tell you whether your benefits are sufficient or whether you should consider supplementing your group policy with individual disability income protection. Protection that is portable, tax-free, has other benefits, and can fill the "gaps" in your group long-term disability benefits.

Your company may also provide Short-Term Disability benefits, which can kick in during the elimination period of your long-term disability benefits. Hopefully, they are with the same insurance company so that there can potentially be a "seamless" transition from short-term to long-term benefits. These policies are especially helpful for employees that are living paycheck to paycheck, and don't have the resources to last for 3 to 6 months of a long-term disability policy.

If you don't have this available, talk to your employer about looking into such a benefit, even if they only want to provide it on a voluntary basis in which each employee can elect and pay the coverage for themselves or decline altogether. Short-term disability income policies can even be obtained on an individual basis, if group protection is not an option for you. The key takeaway here is to review what your needs are in this situation, and take action accordingly.

CHAPTER 12

What about my Professional Association Policy?

Many professions have associations that they can join for continuing education, networking, and resources, as well as answering questions and explaining situations that might arise within their industry. In many cases, it may be a requirement of your profession that you be a member of one of these associations and the you be in good standing to continue practicing your profession. This would then allow the association to review your "good standing," depending upon complaints or other situations that can occur with professions such as Medicine or Law.

Many of these professional associations offer benefits to their members that can be purchased individually or for your group. These disability policies are usually group policies that are owned by the association, not by the individuals when they purchase them. The member receives a "Certificate of Coverage" that reflects the language of the actual group policy, not an actual disability policy.

For this reason, it is important to understand most of the points made in the previous section, "**What about my company's disability policy?**" apply to these policies as well; generally, they are not portable if you leave the association and the premiums most likely go up over time. The definitions of disability may make it difficult to collect a benefit and the benefits can be reduced by other social and even private disability benefits. They may offer some additional benefit options, however the rules for group long-term disability policies generally apply to association policies as well.

Most often, they also include a provision such as, you need to remain a member in good standing with the association in order to keep the certificate of benefit. There may be a provision to allow you to "convert" a portion of the benefit to an individual policy, but this isn't as common.

I recently reviewed an Association Benefit for a client who had many of the benefits and limitations that I have noted in the group and association benefits that we have discussed.

One provision that I found most interesting was that the certificate indicated the member could convert a limited amount of the policy to more limited provisions benefit individually. However, it also stated that this "conversion" could NOT be done if the association decided to change insurance companies or terminate the group policy altogether.

In other words, my client would have to convert to an individual policy on their own volition and without as rich definitions and benefits when they did so. My client didn't appreciate the fact that he didn't own or control his own policy and what happened with it.

One association that I spoke with refuses to make any insurance policies available to their members. When I asked them why, they indicated that when they had offered them in the past, they had trouble if they changed to a different insurance company for their members.

Apparently, the way it was supposed to work vs. the way it actually worked was not explained or understood well enough, resulting in many members of the association that had the benefit originally who were not able to get the new benefit from the insurance company they were changing to. There were still several law suits from members that the association had to deal with. They didn't want any part of trying something new. This was unfortunate for both the association and their members.

97

Again, having the help of an experienced professional agent in these policies can be worth the time and effort to make sure that you have the right benefit for your specific needs in this most important area of protection.

CHAPTER 13

What if I get declined or get an exclusionary rider on my policy?

When medical questions are asked on an application for disability income protection, (or even for life insurance), it allows the company to make sure that it isn't taking on a potential risk for claim that is much higher than what the insurance company can bear.

Insurance companies have actuaries that are specially trained to assess these risks and help a company determine what are and aren't acceptable risks to insure. (If you've ever spoken to an actuary, like I have, you'll understand that it takes a unique type of individual in this field of expertise).

If there is a medical condition, either presently or in the recent past that is outside of the actuarial guidelines, coverage can be declined or can receive a "rider" to exclude or modify the coverage for that specific condition.

If you get a rider on your disability policy it isn't the end of the world. The policy may still be worth purchasing. Here are some significant reasons why:

First, the rider is usually for a specific pre-existing condition only. As we have seen, there are hundreds if not thousands of different causes of disabilities. Like losing one sheep from your herd of thousands, it is a loss but you don't give up on the remaining ones that you have for the loss of one.

Even if you were to have an exclusionary rider and had a disability under that area, I would still encourage you to make a claim. When the claim form is completed there is a part your physician will fill out regarding your specific disability. In essence it asks the doctor if the disability was caused by, contributed to, or a direct result of the condition stated in the rider.

If the answer is yes, then the purpose of the rider is fulfilled. If the answer is no, most of the better disability companies will probably pay the claim. (I never guarantee this, since I am not a claims expert nor do I claim to understand the entire benefits claim process—that could be the basis of an entire book in and of itself)

Even with an exclusionary rider, you are still protected for the thousands of other types of disability. Review carefully the language of the rider as well as the explanation from the insurance company as to how it is specifically applied. An agent with experience with these riders and with the company can be a tremendous help to you here.

Second, the exclusionary rider may be able to be taken off in the future, such as after 2 years in many cases. After a period of time, if the medical issue is resolved with no further treatment, and full recovery is indicated, it is possible to ask for a reconsideration of the rider to be potentially removed.

This usually involves going through the medical questions again, possibly having a new paramedical examination, and underwriting by the insurance company again. If the company determines that this medical condition is no longer an issue there is a good chance it can be removed at that time altogether. If not, the company will not remove the rider, and the policy will remain as is.

It is important to note here that if the company decides to keep the rider the policy cannot be further changed if there is a new medical condition found. In other words, the policy can only get better and not worse, no matter what the new medical questions and exam reveal.

I have a client that was given a "smoker rate" because he used tobacco. I told him, if he would quit and go a year without using tobacco we could do a reconsideration application to have the smoker rate reduced to a non-smoker rate. Almost to the date of a year later the client called me to let me know that he had stopped smoking and wanted to do the reconsideration application.

When the underwriting was completed, the insurance company decided to keep the rider on the policy. The reason, as I explained to the client, was that although it was true he had stopped smoking tobacco, instead he was now smoking marijuana. Since this would not have been a risk that would be allowed on the policy initially the rider would remain.

Since they couldn't change the policy or terminate it now, they could only keep the policy as it was. As stated before, the policy could not get worse no matter what the new situations were. The policy could only remain the same since it could not get better.

The important thing to remember is that insurance companies are not in the business of writing insurance policies that are likely to pay out more than they receive in premiums. Neither you nor the insurance company knows if you will ever have a claim from your specific medical history. They can only go by what the averages show as the probability you will have a claim because of a specific medical condition and treat you the same as they would anyone else asking for coverage.

In fact, you wouldn't want to be with an insurance company that offers coverage to people that are very likely to make a claim soon after getting coverage. Either premiums would have to go up, or the company wouldn't be able to stay in business—leaving you with no coverage at all.

CHAPTER 14

When Should I Discontinue My Disability Insurance?

As I review coverage with clients periodically, to make sure that they still have the proper amount of coverage for their current situation, this question comes up. This brings up an important point about disability income protection. That is, that like other insurance protection, it should be reviewed periodically to be sure that it is still the right amount of benefit for you at present.

It is not the type of policy that, once purchased, you can forget about and not look at for the rest of your career. When someone tells me they have a great disability policy already, I always ask them,

When is the last time you reviewed it to be sure it is still the right policy and benefit for your current situation? If it has been more than a couple of years, I recommend that we review it again.

I have a client who, when they reviewed the coverage they had, found that if they were too sick or hurt to work, the amount of benefit would not be half of what he and his family would need to be able to make ends meet. Above and beyond, it would not pay for any additional medical treatment that would be required by his health insurance policy deductibles, coinsurances, etc. We reviewed the option of getting additional benefits through his existing disability insurance company as well as getting additional benefits through another insurance company, or getting the entire benefit through a totally different insurance company.

Looking at all of your options makes sense with any insurance benefit, as it did for this client. Only then can you make the decision that is best for you.

Wouldn't it make sense to make this decision with a trusted agent that represents not only your existing insurance company but several others as well to get the best unbiased opinion possible?

More specifically to answer the question, the simple answer is that you can discontinue your disability insurance when you are able to retire and not need income beyond your existing resources and that your resources are enough no matter what happens in the economy or to you in the future.

I know a lot of business owners that feel if they were unable to work, their business would be able to continue just fine and that they would continue to get an income the same as before. Yet, if you were to ask them if they could go on a trip for the next 6 months or even a year without any contact with their company, almost all would say they didn't think their business would be the same, financially, without them. (We've already discussed this comment, "As long as I can think, I can run my business" in a previous chapter)

Who would hire, fire, make the executive decisions and make the sales? Who would have the connections the owner used to grow the business to its current situation? Even if it were true that the business could continue fine, how long would it be before the employees started to wonder why they weren't doing business on their own, since they were already working on their own and the owner wasn't there anyway?

For many people, they will continue to work past retirement age because they need the money and can't retire. Even if they are working because they like to do so, the additional income earned is usually not just sitting around doing nothing in their lives. As you near retirement, like all other insurance protection, the determination of either eliminating or reducing benefits is something that is best done in a professional review with a trusted advisor. Disability Income Insurance is not protection that you can get on the internet, look at a spreadsheet, turn in an application, and then not worry about further.

CHAPTER 15

Are there other types of disability policies that I should consider?

The simple answer is yes, but there is a lot more to this answer, depending on your specific situation, occupation, business ownership and financial position. In fact, we could devote a whole chapter to each of these different types of disability protection, many of which most people don't even know exist. I will attempt to give a brief overview of other types of disability coverage available, and ask that you consult a trusted advisor for more specifics:

Business Overhead Expense: When I am speaking with a business owner, whether they have individual disability income protection or not, I ask them this question,

"I commend you for having (or getting) individual protection to pay you an income during disability that will cover your mortgage, food, clothing and other personal expenses. As a business owner, the other big concern is who or what is covering the expenses of your business during that time?"

This is a question that most business owners have not been asked before. They may not even know that there is such coverage available, (I am not referring to the business insurance that covers the office expenses if the office is flooded or burns down).

This disability coverage reimburses fixed expenses at the office, such as rent, lease, mortgage payments; employee income, utilities, insurances, and may even pay a portion of the salary of someone to come in and replace you for a period of time. This coverage allows the business to continue viably until either you can hopefully return to work or find other arrangements, if returning doesn't appear likely. It definitely can put your employees at ease, knowing that they will continue to receive a paycheck during a period that you are unable to work because of a sickness or accident. It may also be possible for the premium payment to be tax deductible, since the benefit is being used for tax-deductible business expenses.

Disability Buyout: It is surprising to talk to business owners and ask them if their Buy-Sell Agreement has a provision if one of the owners is unable to continue due to a prolonged sickness or injury. Even some attorneys that I have spoken to have not made provision for this in creating buy-sell or business continuation agreements for their clients.

One attorney even admitted to me that it hadn't even occurred to them to ask. If there is a provision for this, how will the company fund the buyout of the owner who probably needs the payout more than ever in this situation that could be termed, "The Living Death"? Similar to Life Insurance being used to leverage monies of the insurance company for a buyout, disability buyout provides the benefit to the company for this more likely situation.

Key Person Disability: If you have an employee that is important to the ongoing success of your business, such as a key sales person, innovator, or account manager, you should protect your "second most valuable business asset" the same as you do yourself with Key Person Life Insurance. This policy will provide income to your business while a key employee is unable to work for you. It can even provide the necessary income to the company to allow you time to find the right person and train them to replace the employee long term, so that your company can continue to grow and thrive.

Business Reducing Term: I am surprised how many banks and lending companies require life insurance to protect against the loss of monies being paid back if the borrower were to die, but don't also require disability insurance to pay back the loan if the borrower becomes disabled. This coverage will pay the lender directly in the case of the disability that no longer allows the borrower to work. It can also be a valuable and affordable coverage to pay back a student loan, which is something that you can't even declare bankruptcy to erase.

With the size of loans to start many businesses, and the growing size of student loans these days, not protecting against this probable obstacle to your long-term financial stability is almost unthinkable. Yet again, many borrowers and lenders alike don't even know that this exists. Even more surprising is how affordable this invaluable coverage can be when we look into it more closely.

Guaranteed Standard Issue: Simply put, this can allow you to get individual disability coverage for a specific class of employees, (such as owners/managers, employees above a certain income level, or another specific class of employees), without much (if any) medical underwriting or financials required. It does not and should not be offered to all of your employees; you choose the class of employees that you want it to be for. It can be a great way to recruit, retain and reward specific employees since you are offering them a benefit that they may not have or be able to get otherwise.

A business planning group that I worked with had a majority owner who had a heart attack a couple of years previously, but had not had problems since.

This made him uninsurable for individual disability income protection. Although he had a group disability policy, it didn't provide him with the amount of protection that he needed when and if the time should occur that he needed the benefit. When I explained how he could select the key people in his group to provide a benefit for through Guaranteed Standard Issue, including himself, he was more than happy to provide this benefit for his select group.

Although I thought that he would be the one to go out on disability claim, due to his prior health history, I was surprised when, not a year later, his 34 year-old star managers developed Leukemia. Not only the employee and his family were grateful that they had the benefit that they never thought they would need, the group became even more loyal to their employer from that day on.

Some of these options we have discussed are even available on a group basis. I cannot overemphasize the importance of using a trusted financial advisor who has experience with these different policies and their applications with different insurance companies.

CHAPTER 16

How do I find the right company to get the coverage from?

Whether on an individual or group basis, not all companies offer disability coverage. Many that do offer group coverage don't offer individual coverage. Companies that offer disability coverages may not offer all types of coverage or even be the right option for various types of occupations.

A dentist I worked with recently thought that a particular option he had looked at was his best option. When we looked at all of his options, especially taking into account his specific situation and needs, he was surprised to find that another insurance company offered much stronger definitions and benefits for him, and at a lower premium. This isn't always the case, but it's nice to find what works best for the client, versus the first thing that is presented.

Finally, not all companies have the same financial strength and history sufficient to rely on long term, let alone relying on them to keep rates stable or depending on them to not continually try and terminate legitimate long term claims.

So, how do you find the right company for you? We will briefly touch on several points to consider when looking at disability coverage:

What is the financial strength of the company?

Being with a strong company that has the financial size, reserves and ratings is a good starting point. You want to be sure that the company will be there for you long term. There are several different rating companies:

AM Best, Standard & Poors, Moodys, Fitch, etc that can be useful to look at these factors. Even with this, each has its own rating system and letters used to rate insurance companies. An "A+" may be a high rating with one rating company but much lower with another.

Comdex is a company that has assembled the major rating companies' ratings and turned them into a "percentile rating" compared to other companies. In other words, if a company gets a "90" as a Comdex rating, it means that of an average 100 insurance companies, that 89 don't have as high financial ratings and 10 have higher ratings. This can be a valuable tool to use in comparison.

Does the company give good definitions and benefits for my specific occupation and needs?

Most companies have specific markets and occupations that they like more than others. One company may do very well with certain occupations that another company may not like at all. This can make a huge difference as it pertains to definitions, benefits and premiums between the various companies available for your profession.

It sure made a difference to my dentist client. Even within a particular insurance company, there can be different options for the definitions and benefits available, as well as level vs. graded premiums, (as discussed earlier with my medical client).

Working with someone who understands the "sweet spots" of different companies, as well as the benefits that meet your needs best, can help you make a better decision.

Does the company offer more than just individual disability coverage?

If some of the other types of disability coverage are needed, having a company that does many types can lead to less paperwork to complete, less paramedical exams to do, less places to provide information, and possibly a discount when you have more than one policy with the company.

Be careful though. Just because a company may offer two types of disability coverage you want, doesn't mean that having one with one company and the other with another insurance company may not yield better definitions, benefits and even premiums. Check on your possibilities there. I have many clients that are glad they did, and many who have found the best company, definitions and benefits for their individual coverage was one company, while the best benefits for their specific situation with Business Overhead Expense was a different company altogether.

A helpful exercise for many people is to look at these key points of different companies without knowing the name of the company beforehand. I have presented this to many clients. Doing this removes the bias that they may have for a particular company. Only when they select the one that works best for them do they discover that it isn't necessarily the company they thought it would be.

CHAPTER 17

??? How do I find the right agent to get the coverage from?

With so many things to consider, options to review, and specific benefits to look over, Income Replacement is not easy to just "spreadsheet" or shop online. I'm not sure how the typical busy person can figure out what is best for them, especially when they understand how important the decision is. How can you get the information you need to make the best decision on disability benefits?

I have found it invaluable for clients to have a list of questions that they can ask a potential agent or advisor to help them determine who might be a good agent who can empower them to make the best decision for themselves and not just the best decision for the agent. This is not meant to be an all-inclusive list, but a list of questions that can help you to determine whether the agent has the necessary expertise and experience to help you make this most important decision:

Do you own a disability policy yourself?

Initially, I bought a disability policy because of the good advice of a manager who told me,

"you can't sell what you don't own."

Now, I wouldn't be without my disability coverages, nor would it be easy, if at all possible, with my present medical condition.

If an agent doesn't have a policy of their own, why should they be asking you to get coverage for yourself? It wouldn't seem to show much commitment or belief in the benefit to say,

"Well, I don't have a policy, but you should."

How could they know the real benefits of having coverage or how it works if they were to become disabled, if they don't have a policy on their own life? Better still is if they can actually show you at least one of their disability policies, (and they should have more than one if they have been in the business for much time). The old adage:

"Put your money where your mouth is,"

would seem to apply here.

Do you have a personal experience with disability insurance?

Nothing brings home the importance and value of something more than to have a personal experience with it, either for themselves or someone that they know having a disability and seeing firsthand how having disability income protection has saved them financially. Conversely, how they have been challenged financially for not having it. Having had that type of experience, it becomes a mission and a passion to share their experience with others to empower them to be able to make better choices. That is my reason for being in the business of disability insurance and the main reason for writing this book.

Do you have any designations or credentials for advanced study in disability insurance?

An affirmative answer here shows a commitment to expertise in disability insurance and in keeping current in this field. This isn't just a matter of a general designation, such as CFP (Certified Financial Planner), ChFC (Chartered Financial Consultant), CEBS (Certified Employee Benefit Specialist), or even CLU (Certified Life Underwriter).

These credentials are to disability insurance as a general dentist would be to Orthodontics. They may have some knowledge in the field, but it doesn't mean that they would be the best choice for you or your children if they needed teeth straightening. Would you trust yours or your child's teeth to a general dentist that recalls learning about orthodontics, and believes that they can do the job just fine?

Some examples of Disability Designations are:

119

DIF (Disability Income Fellow), **DIA** (Disability Income Associate), and **GBDS** (Group Benefits Disability Specialist). Like the general certifications, these each have specific courses that must be studied and examinations passed in order to have the designation. They also require experience in the industry and ongoing training. Designations also require or imply a continuing education in the field to keep current in the field of expertise. Just calling one's self a "Disability Income Specialist" isn't a recognized designation, nor does it imply that the person is or isn't qualified to do the best job for you.

Are you a member of an Association that focuses on the promotion and education in Disability?

This is also a useful benchmark to measure the commitment and the ongoing education and training to the disability field. The International Disability Income Society (IDIS) is one of the few organizations that specifically promotes disability insurance awareness, education, and application to not only members but the general public.

How many disability companies do you work with?

It's hard for an agent to help you find the best company and policy if they only work with one or two companies. The "one size fits all" approach never really works with this important protection, as we have seen with previous examples and many different types and occupations of clients nationwide.

How many years or disability policies have you sold?

Experience in working with different people and different policies shows that the agent has some expertise and experience to help you best. Would you want to be the first patient of the dentist who thinks they can do orthodontics? Isn't something as important as protecting your income just as important?

Do you have any clients that you have helped that are on disability claim right now?

I not only gained a deeper respect and understanding of the importance of disability income protection when I was disabled, but more each time that I have a client that has used the benefit and can say how much it has helped them to maintain their financial well-being when the benefits were paid to them. It is one thing to be able to talk about the benefits of selling disability income insurance; it is quite another to talk about the benefits to those who have used it.

Can you provide me with any references of long-term clients?

These should be references that have worked with the agent for a while and can tell you what it's like to work with the agent, how responsive they are to questions and needs down the road as well as how well they keep up with their changing circumstances and changing needs. The agent that is here today and gone tomorrow can help you get a policy, but won't be available when you need them later on to keep your coverage up to date. You are looking for an agent that will be there for you when you need them. Having a team that they work with and staff that supports them is also a big plus in this area.

There are other questions that you can ask if desired, such as, "Do you regularly ask your clients about individual disability income protection?" As well as, " Do you ask them about other disability protection policies that they may benefit from?" Like anything good that you truly value, you want to share with others and help them best. Why wouldn't it be the same with protecting your income?

The most important question you can ask is for yourself: Do I understand the importance of getting and maintaining this most important protection for myself enough to take the time to make the best decision for me and those that are important to me? The answer to this question, will help guide you to do what it takes to empower yourself to make the best decision.

EPILOGUE

Megan's story continues to unfold. This is something that none of us would have possibly imagined for a 31-year old that is healthy and active. Despite the surgery and radiation treatment that she has already undergone and the struggles to recover, her continuing treatment has found that the cancer has either returned or moved into the same areas as they were originally. She continues to fight to recover from this ever-changing enemy to her ability to work and help provide for the family. She and her family continue with the struggles that come from something that has changed the course of their family and their financial future forever. She, as well as I, will ever be grateful for the miracle of disability income protection, and having not missed the almost "Forgotten Insurance."

I would like to acknowledge and thank the **Council for Disability Awareness** at http://disabilitycanhappen.org for their valuable data resources without which, this book would not have been possible. Most of the statistical reference data cited in this work was provided by them, for which I am grateful.

Gregory G. Nelson ChFC, CEBS, DIF

Copyright: 2017

87620903R00078

Made in the USA
San Bernardino, CA
06 September 2018